Dad,

I thought long and hard on what item, what nic-nac, what possession I could give to you that would be special enough, that would be meaningful enough. It took me a while to realice the obvious, time.

So, disguised in this book of canadian poetry, are 3 tickets to a Cirque do Soleil performance, in Montreal, in April. My gift to you this christmas is a weekend together. Until then, I thought you would enjoy this book. It was recently published by one of my editors (who happens to be one of the premiere and award-winning poets in Canada. my favourites are on pages 23 and 49.

I love you.
-Justin

W9-CHQ-486

WITH ENGLISH SUBTITLES

{ CARMINE STARNINO
With English Subtitles }

GASPEREAU PRESS
Printers & Publishers
MMIV

C O N T E N T S

THE KETTLE

Awake in bed, my ear was trained to its tune.
I thought the thing perfect for turning water

to whistle. It had a certain listened-for beauty.
Under tap, the broadcast of its steep-sided shape

filling up. It was old; the sheen scuffed off.
Yet it whelmed its insides quickly with heat.

The handle was always raised for your grip,
so that when steam screamed the spout's note

you could swing it like a censer to the table.
It groomed small appetites: a cup of camomile tea,

or honey, a spoonful, together with lemon.
Now I realize it was a comfort to the sleepless.

Tonight the kettle and I are sadness-bound.
Melancholy's own tin bell, ready to sound.

J U N K Y A R D

Owning nothing, there is, I see today, a touch of those cars
about my life, a touch of decay in that flotsam of chrome

I recognize, demanding a new curiosity, a new eye to roam
chock-lifted hatchbacks and overturned trucks, vans crushed

and strewn on cinder blocks, all that automotive cartilage
and bone, the mounting lugs, drive shafts, and valves, that

high-rise of mess, that pile gagging on its own size, and then
to have the clutter just sit there, so big you feel really bad

for the ground bearing the brunt of it, scattered and busted,
dismantled, maxed-out—everything allowed its hundredth

free-fall into flaw, leather seats with rips whooping open
on white fluff grins, kicked-in windshields, gutted engines,

and hoods sporting splatter patterns of corrosion as bright
as blood, then there's the flacking of mud, and colour here

nothing more than the crash of tinctures. And the surfaces?
Oh, fish-scaled or brindled or grease-charred or scratched

like Arabic scribble, paint the tint of fruit sickened with rot,
dense exfoliate pinpricks of umber that crust lichen-thick,

or ochre hemorrhaging up through some scraped-off yellow.
Then the ground freaked with patches of oil, and, tree-like,

a tall stack of tires black-barked with treads. The air tastes
of it, whatever it is that stains the hubcab's bowlful of rain,

and from deep inside that heap—part Hieronymus Bosch,
part Mad Max—you can hear the ticking of some fragment

expanding as it loses its last faint bloom of warmth. Look,
all these scummy windows reply with a version of myself

peeking into smudge-lit interiors at erstwhile dashboards prinked
with accessories and imagine this '70 Pontiac motoring off

in an open road afterlife—unless, of course, this is it, unless
erosion is a category of endurance, unloved and unlovely,

and the hereafter is simply what remains when you're left
with what survives its subtraction (and what's left is always

some old, odd scotched part—iron-grey chassis, gashed grille,
door frayed off its hinges). Better yet, you'd think all this

would foul a sunny spring day but this junk has lived here
so long beside the half-darkened wood it's now one more

disbursement of nature, the weather taking metal back to its
first motive, becoming a new growth, a small rust blessing.

Scarecrow

Mummified broomstick. God's own grain
become chaff. His dotage a daily coming-to-terms
with the silliness of a straw-packed head
and a broad-brimmed hat. His fearsomeness
wrecked on its stem. Once thug-bodied with menace,
he is a mark of defeat, a flag at half-mast
and wrapped in its cordage. But awake, always awake,
always watching the same leaf flattened
by the same gust against the same barn shingle,
always watching the same weeds, doubled.

O bladderskate, O foolosopher, O blateroon
the birds jeer. The scarecrow is certain the moon
rummaging through his soft chest has sown
some death into him. Stopped clock with its smell
of stale perpetuity, he waits for pitchfork,
plow, spade splitting peat. Meanwhile he learns
the names of wildflowers, and hope is thus
administered by coltsfoot and white cress, by chickweed
and purple loosestrife. That? That's no wind
but him whistling to himself through his teeth.

WORST-CASE SCENARIO POEMS

There are no two things as important to us in life and art as being threatened and being saved. What are ideals of form for if we aren't going to be made to fear for them? All our ingenuity is lavished on getting into danger legitimately so that we may be genuinely rescued. —ROBERT FROST

How to Escape From a Car Hanging Over the Edge of a Cliff

The thing to avoid is a front-row view
of your car taking a rude, impromptu
header into the stones below. So, nice
and slow, ease away from the wheel,

and retreat to the rear, know each new second
the car's braked bulk pauses, fidgety,
on that rock lip, is one less second
to steal. What you want is to open, gently,

a back door and quickly step out, hoping
to heaven you don't hear the awful
creak of your hood nosing down, or look up
at a sky ducking under the suddenly

steepling ledge of your trunk, or feel that free-
fall panic, knowing you're fucked.

How to Climb Out of a Well

Houdini-hug the sides like an upright
L-shaped wedge: back gripping brick,
ass off the ground, legs end-stopping
the other edge. Next retrieve one foot, fix

its heel to your rear, rest on that ledge.
Good. Now place both palms against
the wall behind you, and, seizing all that traction,
make like a bubble in water. Okay, so

the trick's tough. But surely it's better
than your panicky hooting which sets this
ossuary echoing. Otherwise, sit back
and wait, watching the tiny brim of brightness

at the top and the light disappearing
down that dank, grave-smelling drop.

How to Survive a Sandstorm

It's fast. The sky goes dark, then grit
chokes your air and soon every blast
hurts like it's erosively resifting your face.
So think ahead: socks, shoes, pants.

It blows low to the ground. So find, if you can,
a higher place (forget this in the Sudan
where the *haboob* pushes a solid prow
of sand five thousand feet tall). Do dig in, press on

against that sun-obscuring squall, aware
what's unprotected will turn pulverable,
your flesh more grist for the gust. Last,
it's unbreathable. So hold a hankie—best

make it wet—over your nose and mouth,
avoid the taste of your own attrition.

How to Find Water on a Deserted Island

Best bet's at sunrise, when dampness
—rain's dream-self—drowses on surfaces.
What you do is tie a rag to each ankle
and walk through the grass until the sleeping

condensation wakes into the material
to be wrung out. Of course, tarps whose centres
have been staved will also, overnight,
pool some. To go where water hides, think

little-known, think you'll-never-believe-it.
No, silly, not the sea—prey, instead,
on the world's unitemized wetnesses. The region, say,
around a fish's eyes, or a fish's vertebra

—sip from those tiny, tinfoil-hued trays
or snap the spine and suck it like a straw.

How to Survive a Volcanic Eruption

Let's just say that if the falling debris
failed to clip you, and you weren't consumed
to cinders by the lava, and—happily—
didn't give up your ghost to the fumes,

and say the mudslide, the tidal wave,
and the earthquake somehow passed you by,
and at your getaway (a close shave!)
the engine didn't clog with ash and die,

ash which, instead, kept its account
with all those others trapped behind, indoors,
who stared out from their highest floors
at darkening streets turning Pompeiian—

then, ah then you'd be in dumb luck's debt,
your life the tally of what can go right.

The prettiest are hung, framed and flat under glass.
Others you draw down like a big window shade.
A quick tug, and they speed clatteringly upwards.

Of course, a forgotten packet of papers is always
mulling in some sea chest: a booty-print, soiled and salt-chewed,
with an X-marks-the-spot clue. Or this: in 1592,

a Portuguese, kerchief-sized navigational chart
two Dutch upstarts were clapped in irons for trying
to smuggle out. That, by the way, happened a lot.

Half-assed spy plots to unmurk the East Indies
in a tycoon scheme for trade. Portuguese galleons,
bunkers flush with spices, drugs, pearls and silk,

short-cut it home using state-secret Far East routes,
while Europe's direction-baffled merchant fleets
made do with chump-change goods. Those sham sketches,

jerrybuilt from rumour and the brags of adventurers,
reduced a few flag-proud sprints across the ocean
to epic ditherings on endless water, with the crew

scared stiff, adrift in that far-offness, that vast negligence
of hearsay, where each wave logged and ledgered
looked the same. (*No ifs-and-buts about it: we're lost,*

wrote one old salt. *And without the tiniest breeze to thumb a lift from,*
though the hard-breathing sea's stirring up enough
of a draft to fuss with our spinnakers.) But now with

our whereabouts debugged and the world's broad-
backed continents and sickle-shaped bays proofed against paraphrase,
now with bossy street guides telling us where to go

and the sea's cornerless distances feeling much too
fenced, and now that you even see yourself geographically—
a darkened spot experiencing a bout of low pressure

on a weather grid—you want to praise the exuberance
of those early cartographers, praise their whimsy
and wild bids. The guessed-at realms of Frisland, Drogeo,

and Icaria. And depictions which, in their heyday,
were steeped in weirdness: hooved man-monsters with eyes
epauletted on their shoulders, or rocs flying about

towing elephants in their talons, or a race of men
with a single foot the span of a parasol so that *In the hottest season*
of Summer they lie along their backe and defend

themselves with their foot against the Sunnes heat.
And what brought all this to mind wasn't the tale
of that lightfingered Dutch duo or the image of caravels

newly caulked and riding at anchor, clueless about
whatever coastline-connoitering plod they'll soon be
slowed to, but—of all things—your father and his

Columbus-confronting-the-flat-earthers frustration
when pressed with too many questions. "What the hell,"
he'd say, "Do you want me to draw you a *map*?"

THE SUITCASE

was steerage-bound and unliftable
with stowed hope. Put anywhere,
it stayed put. Heavy as Ptolemy's
eight-volume guide to the world's 8000 places.
Barrel-plump, girded and gridded
with twine, it gave off a great hurry
as though it were King Aeolus's valise:
north, west, south and east winds
roofed-in for the ride. Émigré swag bag,
sea-going satchel, abandoned where
it wintered, or set aside for old shoes,
but still champing to be off, brown
relic of durability made indefatigable
with mileage, like a tire worn smooth
but still sound. And never the posh,
wickerwork, brass-latch brand either
—an Oshkosh, a Hatmann, a Wheary,
a Seward—but a no-name garment-drudger,
its leather stained by damp blooms
of salt, and so warped with weather
the grain looks oaken. Open, it smells fumey,
like soil left to fallow after a season
of rain. Tipped, it turns turtle on the floor.
Stacked, it's a plank in a pile shaken
out of true. And upright, it albatrosses on the deck
of an attic, big-winged and hunched.

Or that plain-prose bag dreams itself
a sentry box, a choir stall, a bale of hay,
or maybe, kindled by its testimony
of all that blue, all that water shelved
on water, it dreams its hull into a hinged
basket floating down the Nile, a little
St. Brendan boat steering the promontories.
No. It knows itself empty, long-used,
and outmoded, knows itself one of those creatures
conjured by mapmakers, a grimacing
unguessable thing cramped in a margin,
knows itself much-punished, dun-pallored,
steeped in the practice of persistence

On the Obsolescence of *CAPHONE*

Last heard—with a lovely hiss on the "ph"—
August 1982 during an afternoon game of *scopa*
turned nasty. And now, missing alongside it,
are hundreds of slogans, shibboleths, small

depth charges of phrasing. Like an island-colony
of sea-birds screeching our own special cry,
I recall words all backwater squawk, recall
the curmudgeonly clunk and jump of their song,

a language dying out but always, someplace,
going on, surfacing in a shoe salesman's patter
or a grocer's chitchat, anywhere conversation's
an inventory of old expressions marked down

to near-nothing and preserved past all value,
spoken but never found on a page. Yesterday I listened
to some Italian roofers at work. Their hoots,
guffaws and barkings-down to the truck. It was

buckaroo stuff, their dialect. Barisi, I think.
Eruptive, roguish, and hard-edged —a vigour
any poem would pestle to powder. But in the way
English can, by trumping up a term, pay out

something more interesting than you intended
—turn a smile into a smirk, make geese clack
overhead, or declare a birch's bole drubbed bare
by a storm—immigrant jabber can flush into

the open a new word that shivers in the surprise
and rush of its arrival, like that spurt of wine
my uncle, with a single suck on a plastic hose
threaded into a vat, would draw out, splashing,

into my glass. You *capish*? I say "immigrant"
but, really, what the hell do I know? A bunch
of banked-up bales I was never born to. Hey *stronzo,*
my uncle Louie would ring me early Saturday,

think you can take a little break from slapping
your dick around and help me? He dubbed it
'na giobba, said it'd be *'nu minuto,* but I knew
he'd be exasperated at my speed and call me

moosho-moosh and send me back to my book
—reading was making me too *stonato* for chores
he'd tell my father. Now I harvest my sounds
from men like these, key my jargon to the spontaneous,

try-it-on effects of their speech, diction gutsy
with curses, urge my poems to unschool themselves,
to roughen their step as they tramp and turn
to hoist and stack. No word too proud of its station.

No word dipped in oak-gall and soot. I want
a homemade vocabulary, tough-vowelled and fierce
for the sheetrock they shoveled, and the steel
they bolted with a ratatatatatat, and the bricks

they troweled with a one-on-two-bend-scoop-
spread-tap-settle, and the sledges they whanged! on iron.
For the meals they couldn't cook, but the rabbits
they'd gut after knocking their heads with a cut of wood.

For the plush boat-sized Chryslers they drove,
the two packs-a-day they puffed, and the grapes they grew
in gardens pegged-out with plums and pears,
apple trees grafted with five varieties of apple

and cherry trees spraying the ground with shade.
A word for their conviction that all you needed
was a wrench, a handshake, a little money down.
A word for the ends they never failed to meet

or the way they knew to drive a nail between
the haft's wood and head to rescue a hammer,
or the afternoons when, over espresso, they'd crack
that women need a slap or two, to feel wanted,

or the way they spoke, with mouths awakened,
mouths quickened by the volatile, unprissy,
impurifying syllables of *gabbadosta*, or *scimunito*
or *futtiti* —itself a good word for the situation

(No speak. *Stai zitto.* But me I was too much
of a *chacciaron'* to stop and thus *scostumato*
is what I was called when I was rude enough
to talk back. *Le parole son femmine, e i fatti*

son maschi—words are female and actions male,
and they thought me *femminiello*, a bit faggoty
in my careful, English talk. So what's what?
My cousins ask when cornering me at weddings.

Well, you got gots is what you got. Go *zappa*—
go work in the fields. But I do, my friends, I do,
and I fear that when the Italian in me is done
scything his last square of grass he'll pick up

and go, and the speech I heard and, at times,spoke
will be the silence surrounding all my poems)
that might one day leave my poems illiterate.
I once dreamt of an eloquence like St. Ambrose's,

unblemished and discreet, lapidary and fluent,
augered by a swarm of bees hovering above
his infant mouth. Today, instead, I want my language
bashed to flinders and I will rummage among

its bits and scraps, its dwindlings and debris,
toting up the reusable versus the gone-for-good.
(And *futtiti?* It means ef-you-see-kay-e-dee).
I want to answer noise with noise, to hit upon

subtitles that fit the gist of what I hear. I always
thought of myself as an airborne assumption,
spored here from some other place, now I realize
I'm whatever comes across in the translation.

The Winepress

Hooped in iron, the staves give it a barrel look.
Three legs planted on a patch of shed. An axle in air,
a piston girding a crank, a drilling-rig and spigot
experimentally wed. The handle needs a two-man,
two-handed clockwise push and what was once
squelchingly tread at crude gallop is now crushed.

It was Gutenberg who studied the way the juice,
phrased past constraint, overwhelmed into bucket,
how the screw held the disk, the dole of strength
behind its squeeze, the steadiness and force of the bite.
Then in 1415 he retrofit the grip for moveable type.
He'd tap each letter ready with mallet, sink the tray
until it clenched paper, then lift it on the wet
whiff of ink, the page printed with the turning-spike's
accuracy of compression. (The font? San serif.)

The Jews hewed theirs from rock. I remember ours
as primal, too, a raised-from-the-elements relic
of realness whose hardwood hydralics sweetly
reeked from the grapes g-forced for our booze.
Also good, in the end, for a nice batch of ooze.
Its ungentleness something I'd read about in school:
The angel thrust his sickle deep into the earth,
and gathered the vine of the earth, and cast it into

the great winepress of the wrath of God. Not wrath, but more
like blooms pressed between the pages of a book.

Oh, I can say all this to my uncle, but he could give a shit,
can't read, and what he's learned, reaching down
to scoop away the flattened mimeo-blue husks,
is that one thing is always being wrecked to make another.
Medieval mainstay. Vineyard's own avant-garde.
Once I saw one big as a boat in the keel curvature of its half-ton girth.
How it stood there in high-shouldered farfetchedness!
Nowadays it comes to us smaller: oak crate held
in place with pegs, short slats spaced for seepage.

MONEY

The coin room, British Museum

Their misshapenness strikes the table in tiny splashes,
like still-cooling splatters of silver: stater and shekel,
mina and obol. Persia's bullion had a lion and bull.

Athens an owl, Messana a hare, a jar for Terone, Melos
a pomegranate. Call it museum money, written off
and not expected back—some Ozymandian loose change,

or a bit of dodo boodle, bygone swag, has-been loot,
history's tithe to itself. And God knows after all this
gazing at glass maybe even you mull the quaintness

of things kept too long. But not so fast. This old currency
returns us to first principles, to a time when poverty
had heft, when debt was assigned its correct weight,

spilled metal coldcocking its solid clink against metal,
when taxes, rents and sundry dues were made real
by the real coins that paid for them, knurled and oblong,

dented and pinched, coins that called out your cost
when spoken on scales and so relentlessly palpable
they held their ground as outlaw selves of your reflective tact,

giving the middle finger to poetic truth. They belong
to days before dollars dipped, when it was futile to speculate
on the facts; ingots were unillusionary, would mean

what you spent, and prosperity, like perdition, properly
shouldered its burden, like those last Roman senators
forced to carry their assets in carts. Know what truth was?

Truth was the unapproximating mix of gold and silver
smelted and cast into bars, the alloy hammered flat,
blanks cut with shears, stacked, then hammered again

into circular shape. Now that's genuine, that's proof.
The heat and hiss, the loud crack of tools. When what you earned
was itself evidence of a life lived in labour, the stubble-

to-beard truth of busting your butt—a few, of course,
added bronze to phony the weight, but being neither metaphor
nor symbol, its quality could be checked by a chisel cut.

Never mind it's all junk. Never mind it's all
hauled from attics and hurried out of cellars.
Here the much-used returns as just the thing—
dusty, maybe, age-spored and dank-scented
from whatever dark spot it once slept in, now
awake on tables, each item tagged WORKS
or more sincerely SEEMS TO WORK. The bidding's
rarely prudent—eighty dollars for a cracked
weather-clock!—but in each numbered lot, by rows,
convene perfect little workmanships of ruin,
the dingy, the drab, the gist-of-the-thing, whichever way
newness chooses to phrase its own passing:
brass with its sun-on-gasoline stains, corrosion
typing on copper with its bright green font.
Here bric-a-brac goes from grimcrack to buyable.
Here Constance Marsack's black ash basket
will be loved again, and even the hurricane lamp
last hanging in Frank Spence's fishing shack
gets another, closer look. Scoping out a bargain?
Trust me, Eliza Sifton's tin breadbox isn't it.
Because here the mandolin's missing strings—
snapped during Bobby Agger's last drunken
dockside solo—aren't errors but the very ledger
of its worth. A postcard from the World's Fair, a teak chair,
a kettle's black shell, a bell, a washtub barrel,
a blistered leather satchel. The auctioneer fast-talks

Caedmon's song from these cast-offs, each piece a lesson
on perishability's long patience: the oak stool
Gloria Hulbert used for the pantry's top shelf
distressed to a blossom of scuffs, Dr. Lapington's
seven red hankerchiefs laundered to the clean,
threadbare conclusion of colour, Father Di Piero's
calfskin bible faded to a halftone, a quartertone,
subdividing toward a lingering, sunlight-dwindled ochre.
Truth, here, isn't beauty. Or no, perhaps truth
is beauty, if beauty is the slow, speckled, jewel-tiny
accretion of tarnish. God is in the grit of every
diminishment, even the froth pilling the surface
of those pillowcases the local librarian covets so she can
breathe from the Hamilton's long-married sleep.
Obsolescence will always take you into account,
who live at eye-level with your own vanishing.
And now Ms. Simon steps outside with her prize,
this windy spume-grey day salted-out by rain,
and walks by the hardware store and diner, past
shops in their sooty-roofed, brickwork nuance,
and out along the docks, the rusting oyster boats,
the twitching fish-bone stems of autumn leaves.

A Brief History of Lanterns

Three-quarter peeled, the strip was dipped in fat,
left to stiffen, and the pith lit. Next
they moved your pinch of flame
into a flask, canopied you under
crimped tin, made you weatherproof
and brighter, clean and long-burning, gave you

a kerosene steadiness for the mills
operating late into the night;
sailors performing
duties on a dark sea; doctors
racing their buggies down
stormy rural roads; or just to option

lifting your shine into the iris
of an open moment. As an oil lamp,
you slowed light to half speed,
ceded each inked-in interior
a charcoal-suggestiveness.
Now you print a salt-glare on walls, bleach them

brilliant, your luminosity married
to air chamber and side tube, burner and font.
My dreams bred their own
species: a black corniced box that hung
from the grip of the angel of death
galloping about on a horse. I'd stare

into that furnace-sheen of ash and bone-flecks
and wake up. Part of the mise en scène
of hay-banked fields and steep
coastal cliffs, of locomotives, steamships,
and coal mines, you burned
shadows to an aureate ochre, sent

the dark to a place miles north of our wintering.
Something in our lives your light deferred.
Tucked away as shorthand
wattage during outages, you are now
an ordinary thing,
switched off, in a cabin, while your mind stays

camphine-bright living out its own lantern-days,
spelunking a bituminous secret
sunk deep in the self. Tonight
fireflies are match-spurts touching off wick
after wick of grass, while
I scribble in the margins of *Electric Light*.

Six Riddles

I

Fondle me and I'll chalk your fingers black.
   If I seethe crimson then the more
softly I'm blown on, the brighter
   my arousal. Wet, I hiss.

II

I hatch, wind-spanked, and grow effervescently.
   I'm wet but do not dry in the sun.
I froth on sand. Sailors use "yaw"
    to remember me by.

III

I have the strength to haul a forest's worth of oak,
    yet cannot shoulder the smallest stone.
All things stare down upon me
    and admire their own look.

IV

I move about quickly but have no legs and arms.
    In fact, depending on my size, I either
plumply hop or give a muscled
    leap high into the air.

V

Fleshy and cartilaginous, I can fetch smells
    of soddeness after rain, or the stink
of your own sweat. When sick, I leak.
    Many play with me in private.

VI

I can wear a scent for miles, change the water's
    speed with my mood, or flatten
fields. Windows sometimes
    make me whistle.

A C I T R E Z Z A , I T A L Y

Wind on low roofs on rock.
A cloud-shadow extends its dark acre
across corridors of cypress.

Here each day begins with
apricot carts following the old salt-mule track
to the Maremma marshes.

Stooks docked in a shed,
then the grain's debt spilled
onto the threshing floor.

Learn to appreciate the steep coastal cliffs,
the swales of clear rainwater,
the olive trees left to bush

and at harvest the fruit loosened with sticks.
On a good day you can see
the umber of an iron gate's rust

flaking into doused sparks.
Maybe cuckoos and wild dogs.
A gust blowing down leaves

and a ditch pocketing them.
A sun-bleached basket left out.
Scaled mesh and wet rope

drying on mooring-posts.
Here empty brushwood huts
are important. Also important is a road's

wet, churned-up ruttedness.
And listen! The skrick of crickets italicizing a meadow.
Here every day ends with

wooden ladders brought in
to protect them from mist.
The sea conceding its colour

to the sky's diminishing hue.
Honk of gulls guessed farther off.
Wind on low roofs on rock.

HOMEMADE

Not blackberries, cherries. Not picked,
packed in sugar. Jam jar wrung tight,
left outside forty days. Sugar goes soggy
from sunlight's glassed-in excitation,

conjugates into something spumescent,
weather-churned, barely-seeable-into.
And the cherries? Not fresh, but improved
into a ruder bloom: blood-bright skin

snuffed during the boil of its soakage,
flesh an ossified-pale pink. My whow-balls,
my tipsycakes, my little amber apples.
I spoon up a few. Here, you taste too.

Every morning a birdcall
like a typewriter's clatter,
a constant gunfire-chatter of keys,
then, occasionally, a pause,
then a much longer pause,
followed by another very long pause,
until *le mot juste* is found
(leaf-cheer goes up through the woodlands)
and the fracas of fevered
composition begins again.
Me, I fuss with fonts, laptop plod a line,
look out, askance, hoping
to glimpse the little fucker
malingering in the oaks.
"I don't believe in inspiration,"
Hemingway said, "but if
it comes, it'll find me working."
Of course it will. Meanwhile,
somewhere in these vast
surroundings my slow-flapping
birdself alights, chirpless.

This Is Your Mission

Clouds, thunder and lightning. The flow of water
and blowing leaves. These are the signs by which you're
to take position and set your watch. The ganglia
of fibre-optic moss are now rigged for transmissions.
Reports are to be made daily. A warning: errors in encryption

will seep and spread; observe, at the watermark,
how the stones are stained with them. Maintain
a working wariness. Sources tell us that the mist,
with its ploy of pulling against all five senses, is a trap.
(Ox-eyes are runic pranks and are to be ignored.)

As for the redwood's bark, keep the frequency
of its hue open, so as to catch out enemy reports.
Changes in location for our weekly pre-arranged drops
will be greened to the underside of poplar leaves.
If captured, insist you're just admiring the view.

What I Mean When I Talk About Beauty

I love the orchard and its branchfuls of crop
but what I love most are the apples that drop

and turn so soft they squish under my boot.
White flesh with a wet shine erupts from the fruit.

A luminescence that melts to brown mush,
churning up big beds of decay, feculently lush.

I squat beside roots below the lowest boughs
where memento mori meets Midas and sows

gold ruin in the shade. Call it death, but it's not.
I love the birth of pungent, earth-brewed rot.

Yukon Postcards

I

Each day is a winterward hardening.
Willow leaves browned to a suede sheen.

Ochreous ferns, rust-frail. Frayed bark.
The meadow's aromatic asceticism.

Hedges flecked with frost-charred bric-a-brac
and russet-tinged curios of vegetation.

Acreages brittle in their disappearing berths.
Roadsides darkened by the sputtering

of yellow-wicked shrubs. Before my heart
slows with the fossil ardour of autumn,

the spruce's knothole is aperture enough
to send one last green thought to you.

II

I send you the monkshood, damped
with blue, and red lichen clamped upon stone.

I send you the rain, knocked askew
by wind, and geum seeds adhesively

browsing the bottom of my jeans. I send you the fern's
billet-doux fronds and the sagebrush's

scent, with its off-in-all-directions hurrying.
I send you the goldenrod, its fistful

of hay-coloured trusses tucked fast against
the steep slope. I send you the clouds

far-roofing my day. I send you the black bear, and all
the claw-straked bark he leaves for me.

III

The pussywillow's silver windchime
clatters, the sweet clover is ochre-muted,

and frost stills the bluebell's clapper.
The cinquefoil's five-note canto is off-key,

the larkspur, shy creature, is spooked
into stage fright, and the fireweed's whistle

has been thinned to a bloomless hiss.
Even the sea-susurrus is gone: the wind is

radio static in the trees, whose leaves
find the colour green hard to pronounce.

But in grass that is a tawny stubble of syllables,
forget-me-nots blue-bugle your name.

IV

The aspen grove's own smaller weather.
Its thick-as-thatch roof has hoarded

a little heat, surfeiting the September air
with the scent of thriving wormwood

and wild rose. Everything here is jolted
by the last voltage of summer. Violets

and lupine have lowered their guard,
smelling sunlight in the spendthrift whiff

of this paradise. Maybe I too can stay.
Go, wind, tell her what won't sadden her;

send a breeze cargoed with the aroma
of wildflowers hurrying to live forever.

V

They flapped down as if furtively
inked out of the very dusk. Then I saw

tearing and gulping, meat sheared
from bone, beakfuls of gristle. They picked into

exposed crevices, scissored their way
to the tongue, some squabbled

over a pecked-out eye that had rolled
to the driveway. It was nearly unwatchable,

that collision of ravens with a moose's
hacked-off head. But like good poets

they worried out the extra words all night,
revising life to a clean, white skull.

VI

An overnight storm and the yard
fuggy with mud's pungency. By now

whatever hasn't pooled, urinous,
in the grass' declivities, is slurry

trickling down to the rain-seared
dirt road. I miss you. This damp morning

shrubs lamp the fog: every twig
fletched with a tiny, pentecostal,

phosphor-bright leaf that brightens
when I blow on it. At my feet, the arrested

shimmer of the birch's final colours:
dun, umber, cinnabar, chartreuse.

VII

I send you this bare ridge, stone quay
where the winter wind has moored.

I send you the immense cloud-shadows
darkening the valley floor. I send you

the willows still worded with leaves.
I send you the taste of tarnish in the air.

I send you the friable tufts of sedge
that effloresce into a copper powder.

I send you this cliff, hirsute with lichen.
I send you each crevice's heart-easing

exhalation of stonecrop. I send you the bearberries
incarmining these rocks with my love.

VIII

Should I mourn the yarrow, with its flat
cluster of white flowers vermilioned

to a valedictory hue? Why rue this opulence,
this ferment of new colour? The meadow

nicked with a hundred tinctures of yellow.
Or the apricot glare of leaves which,

netted by underbrush and roadside bushes,
froth in their large, churning numbers.

What else do I have except leaf and flower
steeped and saturating in their lustrous departures?

Sage, willow, bronze-flaked goldenrod.
Each thing verbed into a second bloom.

IX

Yesterday, while sunlight boosted
the low-volume sheen of the leaves

to a bright-as-brass blare, a nippy,
blow-in-your-cupped-hands breeze

revved itself up in the branches.
The gusts caused a huge flouncing,

then a downpour: leaf pleated over leaf
built sheaves of dry deciduousness

that today, sogged by early flurries,
release an uproar of odour. This, too,

my loneliness loots: snow investing some
foliage with the prosperity of a scent.

X

Twig-whiskered, the blueberry shrubs
moat in stanzas of snow, every furrow

fissuring the poplar's bark is seamed
with white, and the leaves spring hammered in

the wind pulls up so suddenly they ring
in the air. If description is an act of love

I record for you fern-roofed orchestras
of white mountain heather with their tiny

woodwind flowers, rearing spruce-root
groined with red sprigs of bastard toadflax,

and, higher up, moss-meshed hummocks
where every open weft is wildflowered.

W H Y ?

There was this cabin in Dawson,
and, oh, the askewness of it. Walls out of plumb,
clockwising off into ground. And *cold*.
Wee chinks in the wood would halt

the wind and forward it on as a draft.
Then the whoosh of air rapturing up
the chimney. Floorboards that sneezed beneath our boots,
and the silty tapwater gave, well, a *richer* sip
than I was used to. Everything once
nailed, fitted, or mortised into place,
slouched. But in the kitchen, up in a corner,

was the most perfectly mated pair of timbers,
the sweetest tangents I'd ever seen,
and I knew that if that shack stood, it stood
because it trusted the temper of that joint.

WEDDING DRESS

White, of course. A veil, certainly
(which I'll lift to the kiss-me
    klaxoning of your lips). What else?
A bit of billow at the shoulder?
Some fluting at the wrist? Though nothing
    too lavish, I would think—you've always
given that posh stuff the runaround.
And then I think neckline
(low, I hope) and how it'll broadcast

your full, bared throat, as well as a bodice
snug enough to vouchsafe a close-cupping hospice
    for your breasts. Then?
Then the dramatic yardage of a trail—
endless sheaves of tulle and satin
    so oxygenated with sheen each flexure and flounce
seems spume. Or no, a lustral truss
swanker and shorter, sexually bold without any
threadful huff. Better still, perhaps

you'll happen across a new heraldry
of nuptial frock, some rare dress
    understudying upon a merchant's stuffed rack
for its one big break. Whatever
you do, funny to think such a made-to-measure feat
    of filigree and furbelow
will only be worn for a day! And when
I imagine you, swathed and pearl-accoutred
in a dress allowed one unduplicatable

passage through this world, I wish … what?
I don't know. Ever hear of Eliza Donnithorne?
    So sad. Jilted in June 1846,
she refused to change into anything else,
and thus whiled away her days
    gussied up *en grande tenue* waiting for her groom.
And waited forty years, never moving
from her room—windows shut, drapes drawn—
until that dress decayed, but still hung

on her body when she died in 1886.
Ah love, forgive me, impatience goads my thoughts
    to such odd places! All of this
to say: I can't wait. But until then my wish
as you stare into that mirror
    is for all *your* wished-for details to stare back,
the wedding dress a second skin you'll
fit your whole life to, as your mother,
crying, zips you—my bride—forever in it.

SONG OF THE HOUSE HUSBAND

Cherish it most when it steams—
"steam," though, fails to praise
its seethe of vapour, or, propped
upright, the suspirating hush as it catches
its breath. Flanks like the shins
of a ship or open halves of a mussel,
and, on its brow, the spirit-level's
impressionable bubble. Fructifying flatness,
it takes my trouser's frown, gives
back pleats. Takes my tired, tucked-in shirt,
makes it newly dapper. And really,
nothing's like the hiss of its hull
kissing a dampened dent (releasing
that rich, road-side scent of rain
on dust). Hope for the linens freckled
with folds. Hope for the crimped,
the crumpled, the crinkled, the crushed.
Hope for the rippled, the ruffled,
the rumpled, the rucked. O coffer
of creaselessness! I do not know
how to cut a straight furrow. I do not know
how to drive a batch of nails. But
grip your handle as I would a spade,
your heft the heft of a hammer.

A C C I D E N T

Hours after our big quarrel, I step out
of my study for a little more coffee,
stop just as you change the channel,
and both of us watch two police cars
cordon off a sunny stretch of road
where a large piece has landed, a piece
made menacing from a bad marriage
of atmospheres. Something went wrong.
The story turned on a disintegration,

and authorities now scramble across
the Texas and Louisiana countryside
for sheared-off, descent-scorched shreds
everyone is warned not to approach.
Late sun fills this room we both love
for its light. On a shelf, our wedding photos.
And all this is one thought—fidelity,
loyalty, trust—and inside that thought
flares another thought of something

smashing against the sky, something
blown asunder, flakes floating down.
As you sit there, waiting for those in goggle,
mask, and suit to spacewalk toward
wreckage shocked into extreme toxicity,

I imagine a young wife this morning
answering the phone, expecting one more
routine reassurance of one more safe
arrival, and is instead sent crumpling

to the kitchen floor. And as I stand here,
too scared to touch those final words
I spoke, I imagine the woman's friend
rushing over to comfort her, and afterwards
how she drives home to her husband.
It's late, but he's still awake, waiting.
One lamp's left on, the children are asleep.
They embrace with fervour and relief,
speak rapidly, interrupting each other.

THE LAST DAYS

And then there were birds inside our dryer duct.
Who'd have thought it fit for sparrows, two,
to be exact, I spied out days ago on the wire
and now, somehow, each brisked past the vent's

narrow neck (no bigger than my thumb) deep
into the tubing, a slimness through which, flattened,
they flowed, all chirrs and wing-whirrings,
as they flew off and returned, flew off and returned

to that fraction-of-a-fraction of a world, that squeeze-
yourself-small chamber. Amazing, that they'd
swap the ampler air for some daylight-snuffing aviary.
Amazing, that they'd trade their sky quiddity

to rattle around like moles in a seam of warm leaflessness,
a constant chirp and fidget I'd had enough of.
But you understood their bivouacking as cute, saw them
as some feathered truism of companionship

convening a valentine in our nook, and refused
to switch on the machine to blast them out, sensing an urgency
in their hurried departures and circlings-back
—carrying, what, twigs, leaves?—and you were right.

Soon there were chick-cheepings, six a.m. medleys.
Soon they were the one happiness in that house,
keeping us awake on separate sides of the bed,
each wondering if the other saw it as a good sign.

One Month Later in Switzerland

I knocked around like a lost tinker,
then stepped into Saint-Saphorin
—straightaway I knew the place

was a find: cobblestone and grey granite,
kiln-dried oak doors and slate roofs
crewelled with exquisite rain spouts,

and how everything snapped shut
in the pleats of alleyways and alcoves.
Fishing village, too, if the fish-stink

meant anything. My point of view,
with its frothing footage of the sea,
told me I was at the top. So I did the descent

and met corridors like brief cliffs,
and squinting stone steps, and walls
that took the turns at short angles.

I climbed down a strata of balconies,
the dampness geologically drawing
from brick hints of soot. That said, it was

a squeeze. Windows eyeing windows,
and cornices and joists in tight truce.
Everything matched up, his and hers.

I continued on, head lowered, alone,
and then, the way sudden sorrow can change
the sense of each detail, I felt myself

abbreviated into those inches, pared
to the bare-fit length and width of whatever
whole and Lilliputian families lived

in all those smartly shelved houses
imprinting my sight with the skyline
of their steepness. Still, I pushed through,

past the elbowroomless doorways
and tea-towel awnings of that flue-tipped republic,
parapet outpost with its bric-a-brac

carpentry, past its painted stucco and clapboards,
its wine casks spigoting from walls.
I kept at it, clocking clear of recesses

and niches, thresholds across which
you'd carry a baby bride, staircases
screwed into the sleeve of that rock face,

hedges cramponned to their soil, air above me
half-roofed by flutings, funny the odd
feelings you get when all you're trying

to do is stay the course, hand-fasted
to brick, steadying yourself against the walls
as if they were a wife; half-crouched

in areas like movie sets too small to use,
and then got to the bottom, breathless,
like that last bit of sand in an hourglass.

And then? Then a chapel. I slipped in.
The place was cool, moreso the pew
where I sat watching dust aerate light

that cast shadows so fine they seemed
nibbed-in on each flagstone's vellum.
At the front, side by side, two empty chairs

I tried to ignore. I left and, outside, met
a man who held a bough-thick broom
with its skirt of birch-spray, and swept.

Good to Go

Small—a runt of a compass, really—with a tiny
bolt-hole hatch I lift on the needle cooped up inside.
The slightest toggle gives it a clock-ticking spin.
Useful for sailors and the sad at heart, all things

unanchored and adrift, all things bobbing in the blank
blue miles of strange southeasternmost quadrants,
new northwesterly latitudes. My marriage wasn't exactly
Here lieth monsters in wait, but more like I'd been

handed an old nautical map with whole countries
included on word of mouth and actual continents
casually left out. The compass was good, yet better
are those nineteenth century matrimonial charts

young grooms perused to avoid hazards like the Rocks
of Inconstancy above the Dead Lake of Duplicity,
and steer clear of —though if you must, make it short—
the Gulf of Self-Love near the Adulterer's Fort.

ONE NEW POEM. NOT MUCH. AND ALL
THE WHILE I COUNT TEN HOURS UNTIL
YOU COME HOME.

One poppy and one delphinium in a vase.
Their orange and blue are flagrant on this dense
grey day at your breast. Did I say "breast"?

I meant "desk". This is about two flowers
deeply staining the air—poppy's petal-phosphors,
delphinium's filigree of flare. Two flowers

high-hatted with light and niched in warm water,
accompanying me a small way into the day.
Two flowers so dazzling they X-ray my thoughts
I grip both wrists and pull you up to squat,

you hunker down … Two tiny skies comprising
a separate weather this overcast afternoon—
their sheen so full of health I feel the stems surge
with colour, then the slickness of our joining.

Summons

Word arrived today from the do-or-die brigade of waves
and the harvest's six sheaves, from the whiff of summer sweat
      and the rolled-up shirtsleeves.
Word arrived today from the grass blabbing green
and the gate's iron cry, from the stonewalling wind
      and the wash parachutingly

pegged out to dry. Word arrived today from the shadow
clocking the clover and the mower's cranked-up music box,
      from the kettle's effervescence
and the tool-shed's broken lock. Word arrived today
from the garden hose revved with water and the oracular
      heartbeat of the empty clay pot,

from the lamp left lit and the well counterfeiting my shout
out of eyeshot. Word arrived today from the breath-clouds
      on the bathroom mirror
and the footprints left behind by the skipping stone's skim
across the lake, from the loud knocks on the squat
      of the chopping block

and the grass chaffy with sprays of flake. Word arrived today
from the sunlight fitting together facets of brightness
       and the new copper penny's
wettish gleam, from the square-stitched span of fence
and the peas pharaonically pouched in their Egyptian dream.
       Word arrived today

from the leaf streaking out of the elm's hanging green
and the week-old housefly misfiring on the sill,
       from the rain applauding
the shed's tin roof and the thunder-spooked collie
tucked into some nook, very still. Word arrived today
       from the fern's capsized

frondful of water and the tick-tock of its drip on the porch,
from the signpost whose wooden leg is booted in mud
       and the mist's moseying
million-legged approach. Word arrived today from the shrubs
winking with butterflies and the tunefulness of thrushs
       shelved in the giant fir,

from the thumbtack clouds which pin the blue sky
to the lake and the bees boozy with nectar. Word arrived today
        from the branch-rigged swing
hanging aslant and the stove-seared footnote on the bottom
of the copper pan, from the rake propped against the lean-to
        and the rust-cankered

watering can. Word arrived today from the shooed-away strays
hightailing it out and the tabby who stayed for one
        last go at the fledgling's breast,
from the gutted carcass with the bones picked clean and the sad
soft-cupped berth of the empty nest. Word arrived today
        from the rungs knuckle-

cracking underfoot as the gardener quick-stepped the ladder
and the at-attention posture of his spade left standing
        in loam, from the shade
reddening the maple's bark to the darkest register of umber,
and the bike's twelve-spoked wheels spinning back even
        as they bear you home.

Acknowledgements are due to the editors of the following magazines,
where a number of these poems first appeared: *Arc*, *The Malahat
Review*, *Descant*, *The Queen's Quarterly*, *Matrix*, *Drunken Boat*
(USA), *The Fiddlehead, Cranks and Lurkers*. ◖ "The Suitcase" was
first published as a chapbook in an edition of 100 by Signal Singles,
Montreal. "At Hawthorndon Castle" was first published as a broadside
in an edition of 50 (with illustration by Patrizia Giannone) by Delrium
Press, Montreal. "Yukon Postcards" was nominated for a Pushcart
Prize. ◖ Gratitude, as well, goes out to Berton House, Hawthorndon
Castle, The Blue Mountain Center, Ucross Foundation, and Chateau
de Lavigny for giving me the time and space to write much of this book;
to the Conseil des Arts et des Lettres and to the Canada Council for the
Arts for financial support. Special thanks to my readers: Pino Colluccio,
Geoffrey Cook, Mary Dalton, Patrizia Giannone, Clare Goulet,
Michael Harris, Marius Kociejowski, Eric Ormsby, Elise Partridge,
Peter Richardson, Norm Sibum, David Solway, Andrew Steeves,
Olga Stein, Andrew Steinmetz, Derek Webster, and especially
Jennifer Varkonyi.   C.S.

ɔ

NOTE ON THE TYPE

Octavian was designed by Will Carter (1912–2001) & David Kindersley
(1915–95). Originally designed for use by Carter's Rampant Lion Press,
it was released for metal composition by the Monotype Corporation in
1961. Octavian's strong capitals reflect a love for letters inscripted in
stone, and its tight-fitting lowercase makes it an economical typeface.
This digital version was released by Adobe Systems in 1990.   A.S.

Copyright © Carmine Starnino, 2004

All rights reserved. No part of this publication may be reproduced
in any form without the prior written consent of the publisher.
Any requests for the photocopying of any part of this book should be directed
in writing to Access Copyright (the Canadian Copyright Licensing Agency).

Typeset in a digital interpretation of Octavian by Andrew Steeves
& printed offset at Gaspereau Press on Zephyr laid paper.

Gaspereau Press acknowledges the support of the Canada Council for the Arts
and the Nova Scotia Department of Tourism & Culture.

2   4   6   8   9   7   5   3   1

National Library of Canada Cataloguing In Publication

Starnino, Carmine, 1970–
With English subtitles / Carmine Starnino.

Poems.
ISBN 1-894031-89-X

I. Title.

PS8587.T3282W48 2004   C811'.54   C2004-902712-3

GASPEREAU PRESS ◖ PRINTERS & PUBLISHERS
47 CHURCH AVENUE, KENTVILLE, NOVA SCOTIA
CANADA   B4N 2M7